LEAVES OF THOUGHT

LEAVES OF THOUGHT

Poetry and Photography by
Mother Ignatius Miceli, M.S.C.

VANTAGE PRESS
New York / Washington / Atlanta
Los Angeles / Chicago

FIRST EDITION

Published by Vantage Press, Inc.
516 West 34th Street, New York, New York 10001

Manufactured in the United States of America
Standard Book Number 533-04041-8

Library of Congress Catalog Card No.: 78-64778

Thinking of You:

To:

From:

Contents

LEAVES OF THOUGHT

LEAVES OF THOUGHT

I turn the pages of my mind
To read the thoughts within.
Then muse; which of these leaves let fall
To share with other men?

ELUSIVE RANIER

Mighty peak, based in clouds.
Head soaring high aloft.
Face shyly peeping
Through the mist.
Elusive, phantomlike—
Deceivingly fragile and sheer.
Describe you? How?
You're here—you're gone—
You're seen—you're not.
Looked for by many,
Found by few.
Yet guarding the city.
A mysterious sentinel
Not often seen by all.

◀ *Mt. Ranier, Seattle, Washington*

YOU AND ME

Hello there!
Can't you see
That you are you
And I am me?

We're both so different,
Yet alike.
Trav'ling our own
Path through life.

So here's my hand
Held out to you,
To tell you that
I'm glad you're you.

I only ask
This, if you please—
Let me be me—
At my own ease.

YOUR SMILE

The day was dark,
The sky was drear.
My heart was heavy,
My eyes held a tear.
I felt all alone,
Without a friend.
Time seemed eternal,
When would the day end?
Happiness had fled,
Joy was nowhere in sight.
I felt life was useless,
Day had turned into night.
I looked up and saw you,
Your smile turned on the light.

THE SEA GULL'S DAWN

Dawn sets you all aglow
As gracefully you glide
Above the sea.
And capture the early morning wind
In your winged arc.

The ocean too
Hoards the morning's light
As its white-capped waves
Recapture the shore
In greeting the new day.

How free your flight!
How free the waves,
Of the incoming tide!
How free and glowing my spirit!
In tune with you, the dawn, the sea.

GIFT

An infant bud
    Tightly wound.
Holding within its heart
    The promise
Of full maturity.
    So small,
        So fragile,
            So like a child.
So much in need of care.
    For only with loving tenderness
Can both unfold—
    From childhood—
        To youth—
            To full blossom.
Petal by Petal.
    Year by year.
Giving of themselves
    For all to see,
The fragrance of their loveliness.
    Sharing what they are,
Helping to brighten the lives
    Of you and me.

TRANSCENDENTAL CONNECTIONS

Like a waterfall, I too leap
Into an unknown deep
To merge in the seething waters
Of a swiftly flowing stream
In search of a quiet, placid pond
To calmly drift and dream.
Dream the dreams I dare to,
Plan the paths I would take.
Lie quiet in the sparkling waters
Of a crystal shimmering lake.
There I would mirror the God I would know—
In tranquility absorb His love.
A love that changes and alters consciousness
Tc a depth words will never know.

◀ *Narada Falls, Washington*

MOUNTAIN TOPS

If I could, you know what I'd do?
I'd climb every mountain I saw,
So I could look on the other side
And see things I'd not seen before.

For from every mountain top the view
Has a vista that's great and wide,
So similar and yet so unlike
The view that is on this side.

I gaze out to infinity
With a joy that uplifts my soul.
My spirit sings, and my heart takes wings,
When I've reached my mountain-top goal.

So, just because the mountains are there
With heads lifted so proud and high,
I'll want to climb to the end of my time,
Or until I'm no longer spry.

INTO THE DARK WOOD

My life's been a roadway
Of ups and downs—
Crossroads, bridges,
Mountains, rivers, streams.

I am now on a path
I must take alone.
So friends,
Walk into the darkwood
With me.

Say not a word—
Hold not my hand.
Let me your presence feel.

I take nothing with me
But myself.
Yet, feeling your presence,
Knowing you care—

Will back light my way
As I, falteringly
Go forward

To the light
Which urges me—
COME—COME—
Be not afraid.

So help me to let go.

◄ *Flying into Seattle, Washington*

GARDENS

I love my little garden,
It's such a delightful spot,
With its pansies, phlox and daisies,
Violets and forget-me-not.

There's a peace that's here in the garden
Where the zephyr breezes blow.
The hum of bees, the song of birds—
Butterflies flitting to and fro.

I think of a Garden's History—
Of when all Time began . . .
And the infinite Creator
Gave the world to man.

God walked with man in a garden
It was there man fell from grace.
It was also in a garden
Where the Savior took man's place.

Christ retired to a garden
When He felt the need to pray.
There in the evening stillness
He'd end a busy day.

In a garden on Mount Olivet
Man betrayed Him with a kiss.
In spite of all man's treachery,
Christ forgave Him even this.

His tomb was in a garden
Behind a hand-hewn rock.
He rose from the dead in a garden,
Giving foes and friends a shock.

It was also in a garden
That He bid His friends good-bye.
They stood there in the garden
As He rose up to the sky.

It's here in my little garden
I meet my God in prayer.
For God must have loved a garden—
He left His footprints there.

◀ *Butchart Gardens, Victoria, B.C.*

STEP LIGHTLY

I ask you
    Walk softly with me
Through the pathways of my life.
    Tread in moccasin feet.
Disturb not the grassroots of my being.
    Reverence the spirit in which I live.

Listen with me
    To sighing winds
Whispering through the halls of my mind.
    Come, play with me
In golden sunshine—
    The smiles of friends I find.

Hold my hand
    When waves of sorrow
Wash over the shores of my being.
    Be gentle with me
When the years of my youth
    Fall like leaves in the autumn season.

Step lightly,
    Touch gently.
Bruise not my inmost heart—
    And I in turn
Will value you
    For the kind of friend you are.

◀ *Aspen, Colorado*

MUSING BY A WATERFALL (SNOQUALMIE)

Rushing waters speak to me of death and resurrection.
Roaring, spilling, descending
Into unknown deeps below.
Decisions made—leaping the cliff.
Eddying in turbulent pools of trial and error.

Rushing waters speak to me
Of days I've let go by—
Decisions I feared to make—
Paths I would not choose—
Dreams I dared not hold.

How like the life of man—
Its ups and downs—
Its leaps and bounds—
Its storms and calms—
Its flow to placid pools

Yet, both forever onward flow,
Each straining towards its final end.
Merging immanent with the ocean's waters,
Transcending time, space, universe,
Toward the known and unknowable God.

DAY'S END

Night falls
Not like a shade pulled down
Depriving day of light,
But softly,
Creeping slowly, gently.
Shading the sky
In rays
Of twilight's glowing colors.
Peace falls.
Tranquility pervades
The sea, the land, the sky.
Christ's Sacrament to me.

◀ *Icicle Creek, Washington*

Puget Sound, Seattle, Washington

CAMP FIRES

Blazing logs,
    Their friendly glow
Lighting the dark corners of night.
    Crackling sounds,
Piercing surrounding solitude.
    Drawing forth from glowing embers
Memories of other fires,
    Other friends.
Warding off the chill of loneliness.
    Flying sparks,
Sending forth pinpoints of fire.
    Telling all—
Companionship and love
    Are gathered here.

◀ *Mora Campground, La Push, Washington*

MY WOODLAND PATH

There's a path that leads
Through a shadowy wood,
Where my footfalls
Are hardly heard.
The breeze, a sighing whisper,
Accompanies the songs of the birds.

The needles of pine
Are soggy when wet,
And slippery when they're dry.
The meandering stream
Speaks aloud in its dream
Of the places it's wandered by.

I walk full of wonder,
With a heart filled with awe
For the beauty surrounding me.
How I wish that this peace
'Neath these trees would not cease,
But through life, my companion be.

◀ *Little Eight and One-half Mile Lake, Washington*

GIVE ME A DREAM

Give me a dream to dream
When Life grows cold.
Fill it with memories
For when I grow old.

For the years will speed away
As you know they must.
And all who ever lived
Will return to dust.

But when my youth has fled
And old age comes—
My stumbling, falt'ring feet
Out of step with Life's Drums—

Give me a dream to dream
Of years gone by.
Light it with memories,
Enough till I die.

The mem'ry of a smile,
A laugh, a tear.
A friendly hand held out
To give me cheer.

Words that eased a heartache,
A look, a sigh.
Just a gracious greeting,
As I passed by.

The sound of children's feet
Up to my door.
Joyful, youthful voices,
I'll hear once more.

Cheerful, friendly faces,
I'd see again,
And hold them in my dream
Till my time's end.

So give me a dream to dream
Each passing day.
Don't let me wait to die,
For my Mem'ry Bouquet!

MY WISH

May the Beauty of all I see
Bring out any Beauty in me.
And may all I say and do
Bring out the Beauty in you.

WONDERING

The ocean's waters are blown by the wind.
Tides change by the pull of the moon.
The sun exerts its force on the earth
Yet all's in perfect tune.

The planets influence each other,
And so all the heavens go.
While here I sit on the top of a hill
And wonder why this is so.

If the earth were much closer to the sun
We'd all burn to a blackened crisp.
However, if we were farther away
We'd all end up frozen to death.

They say the Sun's just a medium star—
There's millions much bigger and brighter.
And each of those pinpoints that light the night's sky
Are light years away, and I keep wond'ring—Why?

We're traveling at such a marvelous speed
Through this spacious universe.
Yet I don't feel a single thing
I wouldn't know if we went in reverse.

There's so many things I wonder about
That are up in that canopy of blue.
I'm glad I don't know all the whys—
I like to keep wond'ring—Don't you?

I'm afraid if I lose my Sense of Wonder
Life would become dull and dry.
My Spirit would shrivel—my eyes grow dim—
If I stopped wondering—Why?

GREEN TOWERS

Tall, majestic, mighty—
Tops swaying in the breeze—
Flashes of the sun's rays
Glancing through your branches
And bouncing off the green below.

Lush the undergrowth—
Shelter for nature's communities.
Mirroring the shadows
Cast by the length and breadth
Of your tall timbers.

Somber at times—
Dark shadows dank and drear.
Moaning winds,
Sighing, sobbing breezes.
A true forest primeval.

◀ *Eight and One-half Mile Lake, Washington*

FROM A HILLTOP

I love to sit and watch the wind
Send fox'tail grass a-billowing.
See the cloud shadows dot the hills
Hear the different songbirds "trillowing."

It brings back memories I have
Of a place I used to go
Where surging waters of the sea
Swept over sands as white as snow.

The restless ocean touched the sky
And hid all else from view . . .
As though there were no other world
But the sea and sky of blue.

When the wind sweeps over the meadow grass,
There's a surge and swell like the sea,
As each swishing, swashing, swelling wave
Crashing over the sands to me.

But here, looking out over the mead below
There's much more of the world to view.
The hills, the pastures, trees and sky . . .
With a breeze that's soft—it's almost shy.

It inundates the hillsides green
Leaving peace and serenity.
How diverse—yet—alike the turbulent sea.
What a different mood it instills in me.

◀ *Aspen, Colorado*

"HAVE DOMINION OVER"

O God! Creator of all!
The beauty of Your creation
Never ceases to arouse my wonder.
Yet, greater still is my amazement
At the knowledge
That all is Your gift to me.
"HAVE DOMINION OVER" You said,
So, in my hands I hold:
The glory of the Universe.
The majesty of the mountains.
The splendor of the sea.
The fragility of a flower.
The welfare of my neighbor.

Have You not also said:
"Whatsoever you do to others, you do to Me"?

Help me then, to handle Your gifts with care.
Grant that I may ever walk in the paths of
Knowledge and Wisdom,
Ever using my Stewardship in cooperation
With Your Creation. AMEN.

◀ *Aspen, Colorado*

IF I WERE A BIRD

If I were a bird
Sitting high in a tree,
Do you know
What I would do?
I'd whistle at every
One I saw.
I know I'd
Whistle at you.

I'd put in your heart
A sprightly tune
That you could
Whistle all day.
Then, maybe the cares
Of Life would lift
And your blues would
Scamper away.

I'd make this world
The happy place
That it was
Meant to be.
That's what I'd do
If I were a bird,
Sitting high in a tree.

TO KATHY

A Promise made is one that must be kept,
Else to ignore one's given word
Would be to lose One's self-respect.
This loss of self-esteem's more drastic still,
For through such remissive loss,
One's own dignity is nil.
It's not that we puff up with self-conceit,
Each time we put to act our given word.
It's just that with ourselves we needs must live,
And it's through our deeds that our true lives are heard.

EXAMINATION

"Do unto others," the Lord teaches us,
"As you would have done to you."
In the light of that message
My day mirrors back
My acts from a different view.
So Lord! Stay by my side
As each tomorrow comes—
Lest I slip back into me.
Not giving a thought—
Putting others at naught—
Being too busy—
Too selfish to see.

REGRET

As twilight slips its cover over day
And sunset slowly fades,
I watch the city lights
Vie with the stars.
How sad to know
As brighter earth's lights glow,
So that much dimmer grows the stars'.
I miss their density
In the blackness of the night.
I ache to see them
Fading from my view.
For, city neons
Can't inspire me
As the starry heavens do.

TOMORROW

"Tomorrow," she promised her conscience—
"Tomorrow I will be good."
"Tomorrow," she promised her conscience—
"Tomorrow I'll do as I should."

Tomorrow—Tomorrow—Tomorrow!
Gee! Isn't it a shame!
You see, she died today.
Tomorrow never came.

FAR OUT

If I were sitting up on a star
Looking down on this planet so blue,
What would a rainbow look like?
Would a sunset change its hue?

Would I be able to see through clouds?
Would the grass on the hillsides look green?
Would oceanic waters
Look turbulent or serene?

Would mountains still look so proud and high?
Would the rivers run silvery bright?
Would Man's work upon the earth
Show intelligent foresight?

Would the difference in the atmosphere
Distort or enhance the view,
If I were sitting up on a star,
Viewing all the earth and you?

◀ *Grand Canyon, Colorado River*

ORCHESTRAL TREES

Golden greens proclaim to all
That Spring is on its way,
As tiny buds on trees break through,
Impatiently to play.

They yearn to flutter and to dance,
To swing and swirl and sway,
Rollick and gambol in the breeze
Throughout a summer's day.

Lo! Listen to the windward sounds,
As each in turn takes part
In Mother Nature's Orchestra,
With leaf and twig and bark.

Soft, soft, the breeze will sometimes blow
And barely move the leaves,
While they in turn with muted sigh
Hang loosely at their ease.

They go from softly sighing sounds
To rushing waters roll,
Then soften to a whisper
At noon's Siesta Call.

You'll hear the sound of cymbals crash
When winds the branches break.
Then with a thud they'll tumble down
The roll of drums to make.

They'll thunder, twirl and havoc raise
Before a summer storm.
Then lazily they'll settle back
To let the droplets fall.

Hie! Come with me to forests green
Where wind and trees keep pace,
To windward harps that sing through leaves
Of gleaming emerald lace.

◀ *Rain Forest, Washington*

A NEW DAY

I woke up to a new day,
I saw a new sun arise.
I woke up to a new day,
Sunbeams dancing in my eyes.

Rosy clouds floating in a sea of blue,
Rainbows playing hide and seek in morning dew.
OH! What a glorious new day!
I'm so glad to be alive.

What will this new day bring?
What new hopes? New fears?
While I sit wondering:
I muse on days passed into years.

I think of the many new dawns
That I've seen come and go—
Of the many new horizons
Ablaze with the sunrise' glow.

Each new dawn brought a gift of time
In which to live life anew.
Time to make many new friends—
Old friendships to renew.

Time to dream new dreams,
The old ones to fulfill.
Time to ease another's heartaches—
Be prayerful—and—be still.

Oh! What a world of wonders
Each new dawning brings!
Oh! What a precious gift Time is—
With gratitude my heart sings.

As Dawn blossoms into a full blown day,
I marvel at wonders yet to be—
And ponder when evening sunlight fades,
If the dawn of another day I'll see.

◀ *Colorado Springs, Colorado*

Cabrini Shrine, Golden, Colorado

SLEEPY LAD
(To Timothy)

I watched your head
Bob up and down.
Your eyelids slowly close.
Yet sleep you fought
And really thought
You hadn't even dozed.

"I'm not asleep," you told me,
Giving your head a shake.
"I'm just resting my eyes—
I'm really wide awake."
Suddenly, no sound was heard,
You toppled on your side.
Just a very tired lad.
Sleep could not be denied.

BLUE SHADOWS

Blue shadows, blue, blue shadows
Hide the sun from my view.
Blue shadows, blue, blue shadows
Increase my longing for you.
I'm crying, I'm sighing . . .
And I'm wondering why
There are blue shadows
Blue, blue shadows—
Hanging over my sky.

Blue shadows, blue, blue shadows,
Hanging over my sky.
Blue shadows, blue, blue shadows
So thick I want to die.
Heart aching, heart breaking:
You're gone and now I know why—
There are blue shadows . . .
Blue, blue shadows—
Hanging over my sky.

WINTER'S PROMISE

There are little brown buds
On the trees in my yard.
They grow fatter every day.
They're telling me—
"Though Winter seems long,
Spring is on its way."
They'll soon burst out
Of their jackets brown.
The green will soon break through.
Though winter shows
No visible sign,
Life will
Spring forth anew.

SPRING RAIN

There are raindrops
On my window
Slipping slowly
Down the pane.
Each speaks to me
Of future joys
That follow every rain.

Here's one that holds a rainbow
These are daisies fair.
Violets, pansies, bridal wreath
Daffodils sprightly and gay.
Each tiny drop
That trickles down
Brings me a Spring Bouquet.

A SEA GULL'S REVERIE

I fly into the morning sun,
    Its warmth aglow
Upon my wings—
    To ride the wind
Out to the Sea.
    To dip,
        To bank,
            To glide.
Skim o'er the waves,
    Ride their crests—
Walk in the soft sand.

    Yes, Scavenger am I—
Gleaning man's refuse
    From beach and sea.
But! Look beyond my purpose—
    For Grace and Beauty
Are also my destiny.

◀ *Pacific Ocean, Washington*

TO A SNOWFLAKE

So soft a flutter through the air,
Leaving neither whisper, nor sigh of breeze.
Gently tucking the sleeping earth
In your white eiderdown, with ease.

So tenderly you wrap each blade,
Each sleepy bush and tree,
And bid them rest in sweet repose,
Till wak'ning Spring call reveille.

In just such gently soothing form,
Each snowflake of God's Grace
Yearns to enfold men's aching hearts,
'Neath coverlet of His Embrace.

For He too had a human heart,
That once bore all men's woes.
He bids us come refresh ourselves,
In Him, find peace, hope and repose.

PRECARIOUS PERCH

Hello! little bug,
Sitting on my finger.
You should take your leave,
Yet, somehow you linger.

Is it you're afraid
To wing up and away?
Or, do you just like
On my finger to stay?

It may be you fear
Human feet as they pass,
While you take your rest
On a thin blade of grass.

You know, little bug,
I must let you go free.
So, go make your home
On the leaf of a tree.

I'll set you up there
Out of human harm's way.
I can't guarantee
Birds won't make you their prey.

OUR LEGACY

Thank You, God! For letting me live
In a world where the sky's still blue.
Where dewdrops gleam on grass still green
And trees are emerald hue.

Where songbirds greet the early morn
Sparkling waters sing.
Nature's wildlife lives serene . . .
Field flowers their joys still bring.

For Creation saw a gleaming jewel
Amid its myriad stars.
Man, it seems, sees just a place
To leave his fuliginous scars.

For the flotsam and jetsam he leaves on the trail
As he travels his way through life,
Mar the beauty and glory of the earth
Endangering all forms of life.

So let us heed God's own command—
Accepting the mast'ry He gave
To us of the sky and sea and land
Lest we make of our earth a grave.

A grave where the birds no longer sing—
Where the trees and grass sear brown.
Deleterious waters can never bring
Needed life to the home of man.

So let us live our Stewardship
Each day with this in mind . . .
Unless we adhere to the Creator's plan
A poor legacy we leave behind.

For we mold man's future on this earth
With our deeds of the present day,
And no gold or silver we leave behind
Will erase our follies away.

So let us leave each place we've been
A little more beautiful to see.
Then, those who inherit the fruits of our stay
Will enjoy a True Legacy.

Marble Head Campground, Washington

BETRAYED

I called you "friend."
At least, that's what I thought you were.
All through the years
I hoped, trusted, tried hard to disbelieve.
I thought, this cannot be.
My friend would not do this to me.
But now—I know.
Your small deceits,
Your subterfuges,
Innuendos—lies—
Pile up so high
The scales are off my eyes.

What was there you expected of me I did not do?
How had I failed you?
What wrong had I done?
Did I cause you harm?
Was my friendship of so little worth?
Christ tells us:
"If someone strikes your right cheek,
Turn your left for a blow also."
How many cheeks did you think I had?
Ceasar had his Brutus—
Jesus His Judas—
Alas! My friend! I had you!

◀ *Snowmass, Colorado*

THE NIGHT SKY AND ME

The night sky deepens each luminous glow
Of tiny, pinpoint stars.
The air, so rare, seems to bestow
A halo to planet Mars.

Venus gleams in a shimmering mist,
Withstanding Orion's glare.
The Milky Way provides a path
Where the Pleiades may fare.

Leo the Lion does not roar,
Nor the Dogstar Sirius bark.
But Cassiopeia still sits by the shore,
While Polaris sends out its spark.

As evening falls around me
And the Alpine glow disappears,
I lift my eyes from the darkened earth
Up to the heavenly spheres.

I sit and marvel at the canopy
Of gold dust sprinkled in velvet blue.
Here in the intensive stillness,
I think my God of You.

I know I'm just a Miniscule,
That my humanity will fade.
But I have my Creator's own Word—
"I am fearfully and wonderfully made." (Psalm 39)

NATURE'S BOOK

I sit on Mother Nature's Lap
And read from the book she spreads.
To marvel at all the tales she tells
Of Her many years that have sped.

Her tales are told in the layers of earth,
Rocks, animals, plants and sky.
I'm agog at how She's carried on
Still beautiful in our eyes.

Her beauty is seen in little things,
A flower, bird, rock or seed.
Her changeable moods are everywhere
Each catering to man's needs.

Her hillsides dotted among the green
With blossoms of many hue
That feed the tiny insects,
Or sparkle with morning dew.

Her forests of many different trees,
Her canyons deep and wide . . .
Rivers that flow at a rapid pace,
Or those that seemingly glide.

Mountains that hide their heads in mist
Or blanket them in snow.
They turn from rose to purple shades
Or frame the Alpine Glow.

The different kinds of clouds she forms
At different times of day,
In skies that go from balmy blue,
To a raging sullen gray.

She keeps on painting different scenes
Throughout the universe,
Constantly dazzling all men
Who inhabit this planet earth.

Yes, Mother Nature's truly wise
And beautiful to see.
But wiser and more beautiful still
Is the God who made Nature Be.

Colorado River, Grand Canyon